For you!

This book will help you to explore language – sometimes in
a group, sometimes with a friend and sometimes by yourself.
You will be:

looking

talking

reading

listening

writing

PRICE

Where you see this sign
it would help to use a
cassette-recorder.

When you have finished
this book, you will
understand a lot more
about your own language
and how you can use it.

1

BLACK'S LANGUAGE PROJECT
Language development for 6–13 year olds

Level 1
For 6–8 year olds

By Pat Craig-Jones
Dodos and dinosaurs
Cat and all that

By Frank McNeil
Broomsticks and bonfires
Goodies and Baddies

Level 2
For 8–13 year olds

By Frank McNeil and Neil Mercer
Here I am
Language around us
Talking and feeling

In preparation
By Jane Hislam and Neil Mercer
Myths and legends
Out and about

Published by A & C Black (Publishers) Limited
35 Bedford Row, London WC1R 4JH
© 1982 A & C Black (Publishers) Limited

First published 1982
Second impression 1985

ISBN 0–7136–2174–5

Filmset by August Filmsetting, Haydock, St. Helens
Printed in Hong Kong by Dai Nippon

Acknowledgments
The authors would like to thank Sue Wagstaff without whose help and contributions this book would not have been possible.
The authors and publishers would like to thank the following teachers and advisers for their comments on the material:
Carolyn Adams, Alison Burgess, June Burrows, Pat Craig-Jones, Bridget Goom, Steve Hoyle, Penny Lumley, Neil Parr, Sue Toogood and Eric Ward. In particular, the authors and publishers wish to acknowledge the invaluable help of Ishbel Fraser, adviser for Lothian region (Scotland) and Jane Hislam primary teacher for English (Leicestershire).
Thank you also to all the children who tested the material, particularly the children of Class 1, St Thomas' primary school, North Kensington, London.

For permission to reproduce copyright material:
Penguin Books Ltd. for the poem *The Queer Moment* by Brian Lee from his book *Late Home* (Kestrel Books 1976) p. 39 © 1976 Brian Lee; Harvey Unna & Stephen Durbridge Ltd. for the extract from *Something in the Cellar* © Rosemary Timperley; R. Chetwynd-Hayes for the extract from *The Cat Room*; Batsford Academic & Educational Ltd. for the untitled poem on page 13 from the book *Creative Writing for Juniors* edited by Barry Maybury; Paddy Kinsale for the poem *Night Shapes*; William Heinemann Ltd. for the story *The Headless Ghost* from *Ghost Carnival* by Aidan Chambers; The estate of Ogden Nash for the poem *The Wendigo*; Bill Naughton for the extract from the book *One Small Boy*; The Arts Council of Northern Ireland for the poem *18A* by Kathleen Allen from the book *Under the Moon, Over the Stars*; the publishers of *Six O'Clock News* by Tom Leonard; Scouse Press for the dialect collection by Frank Shaw; Sangster's Bookstores Ltd. (Jamaica) for an extract from the poem *Bans O'Killing* from the book *Jamaica Labrish* by Louise Bennett; Elaine Slater for the poem *No Buts* from the book *Ways of Talking* edited by David Jackson and published by Ward Lock Educational; Clive King and Puffin Books (Penguin Books Ltd.) for the extract from *Stig of the Dump*; Routledge and Kegan Paul Ltd. for extracts from *The Heroic Book of Failures* by Stephen Pile; Macmillan, London and Basingstoke for the poem *Death of a Cat* by Anthony Thompson from *As Large As Alone* by Chris Copeman and James Gibson; English in Education (NATE) for the poem *Rock our Dog* by Nicholas Hadfield; the Inner London Education Authority for the poems *Poem, Silent Planet* and *Walking in Space* reproduced from the book *Hey! Mr Butterfly*; Pauline Bailey for the poem *The Burial*; Oxford University Press for the extract from *The Trouble with Donovan Croft* by Bernard Ashley (1974); Walker & Co. Ltd. (New York) for the extract from *The Heavenly Host* by Isaac Asimov. Text copyright © 1975 by Isaac Asimov. Illustrations copyright © 1975 by Bernard Colonna.

Every effort has been made to trace and acknowledge copyright owners. If any right has been omitted, the publishers offer their apologies and will rectify this in subsequent editions following notification.

Contents

Feeling scared

With a friend, each make a list of all the things you are both scared of. Put your list into a notebook. Keep all the work that you do on this section in the notebook.

Talk with your teacher and other friends about what frightens them.

When you go home tonight, ask each person in your family what frightens them most. Make notes and take them into school. Talk about your notes with your class and teacher.

Look up the word *fear* in one or two dictionaries to see how it is explained. Write out your own definition of feeling scared.

How do you feel?

In this poem by Brian Lee, the writer describes how he feels when he is scared.

The Queer Moment

It was a queer moment when all on my own
   I woke up in the gloom
To hear, far away, the bell of a church,
   Go boom, boom, boom.

It was a queer minute when something in the walls
   Scampered and scampered, on and on,
And the wind wimpered about the house
   Please, please let me in . . .

It was a queer hour as I listened to the clock
   Tick tock, fidget on the wall,
And my breath wouldn't come, and my heart knock-knocked
   For no reason at all.

And this is how some children described how they felt when they were frightened:

Here are some of the physical effects of being scared:
increased heart rate; increased blood pressure; sweating (often called a "cold sweat"); increase in eye pupil size; release of a chemical called adrenalin into the blood stream which makes you feel excited and tense.
Discuss these with your teacher and then draw a picture of yourself to show what happens to your body when you are scared.
Think about how your pet reacts if it is frightened. How do other animals show fear?

I go all cold and my heart thumps very quickly.
My eyes bulge. My legs go shaky. I get butterflies in my stomach and my teeth bang at each other.

I have an empty feeling in my stomach.
I bite my nails and I have a lump in my throat.
I shiver and shake and I get a funny feeling down my spine.

Let's act

Working with a friend, choose one of these situations to act out.
Use your voice, body and face to show how you feel.
Take it in turns to be the person who is frightened.
Afterwards, discuss how you used your body to show fear.

1 You have broken a window in the house or flat next door. Your neighbour is very bad tempered and you have to go round and apologise.

2 Your mum bought you some new shoes at the weekend. On Monday you leave them at the swimming baths. You have to tell your mum and you know she will be cross.

3 Your teacher gives you all the dinner money she has collected to take to the headteacher. On the way, you go to the toilet and someone takes the dinner money tin. You have to explain what has happened (either to the head teacher or your teacher).

Write a story

About a real time you were scared.
How did you feel?
Where were you?
Why were you scared?
Read your story to a friend.
Was your friend frightened too?
Did your voice sound scared or creepy?

Ask your teacher to choose the six most frightening stories in your class and get the writers to record them on a cassette. Perhaps there are noises and other sound effects in the stories which the rest of the class could also record, like a creaking door or a loud bang.
You will now have a collection of stories you can listen to anytime you want – if you dare!

Being brave

We often imagine that we would be too scared to act in an emergency but these children weren't!

They each won a *children of courage award* for their outstanding bravery.

Look carefully at the way each report is written.

Tracie Cannon, 14, Buckinghamshire

Although she had only just learned to swim, Tracie Cannon of Marlow, Buckinghamshire, did not hesitate when her sister fell into the Thames and sank into 12 feet of water. Tracie dived in. Holding her sister, she swam to a nearby boat and urged Sarah to hang on until their father, PC Dennis Cannon, went to their aid.

Hannah Mornement, 10, Surrey

Arriving home at Ashtead, Surrey, after a visit to her mother in hospital, Hannah Mornement and her father disturbed a burglar. On seeing Mr Mornement stabbed repeatedly by the intruder, Hannah rushed to his rescue and most likely saved his life. By kicking and hitting the knifeman she forced him to stop and run away.

Nigel Box, 11, Wolverhampton

In saving a baby's life, Nigel Box, of The Scotlands, Wolverhampton, almost lost his own. He snatched the two-week old child and its pram from the path of a car that had mounted the pavement. But he was trapped, seriously injured, under the wrecked vehicle. Though it took rescuers an hour to free him, he stayed cheerful throughout.

Choose one of these children and imagine you are a newspaper reporter who just happened to be at the scene when the incident happened. Write a report for your newspaper and provide a headline for your report, too.

Write a story

About a time when you were very brave or about a time when someone you know was very brave. Make up a title for your story. Read it to a friend.

Things which go bump in the night

Here are the beginnings of two stories. Read them carefully and then finish them off in your own words. Afterwards, read your stories to other people in the class and see how their endings are different.

Something in the Cellar by Rosemary Timperley

Ben woke suddenly in the night. A sound had wakened him. But what? All was quiet now. Then the sound came again, a long drawn out moan. And it wasn't coming from his parents' bedroom but from downstairs – or from lower down still.

He sat up in bed and stayed tense, listening. The moaning sound came again. It was more an animal than a human cry, he thought. But what animal? They kept no animals in the house, yet the noise was definitely inside rather than outside. He would have been frightened if it had been a fierce, angry sound, but it wasn't. It was pathetic, packed with sorrow and pain.

Silently he slipped on his dressing-gown, left his room and crept down the stairs, avoiding the last stair but one, which creaked – he remembered that from occasional night raids on the biscuit tin.

He went into the living-room. Nothing there. Nor in the kitchen. He pinched a biscuit and munched it. Had the sound been some sort of dream after all? No – there it was again – louder than before – and it seemed to be coming from beneath his feet. From the cellar?

Ben hardly ever went into the cellar. It was only a mucky old place where the coke was kept. His father went down there at regular intervals to collect buckets of coke, grumbled, stubbed his toes and made a lot of noise. There was no light down there, which made things more difficult, and he'd never bothered to fix one. He was no handyman.

Now Ben wondered if someone or something had got shut in and was wailing to be let out, for the door was locked, with the key left in the lock on the outside.

He tiptoed to the door and put his ear to it.

The next story is about a girl called Sabrina.

She and her family have just moved into a cottage which used to be lived in by her great-uncle, before he died. Sabrina's bedroom is covered in wallpaper with black cats' heads on it. Sabrina likes the wallpaper but it gives her mother the shivers.

Sabrina woke up suddenly. One moment she was in a deep, dreamless sleep – the next wide awake, every sense alert, trying to determine what it was that had disturbed her. She raised her head and looked across the room. A full moon had transformed the window curtains into a silver screen, made the darkness retreat into corners, created slabs of shadow that lay before the bookcase and wardrobe, and turned the dressing-table mirror into a vast gleaming eye. A night breeze crept in through the partly open window and stirred the curtains, making it seem as if all the cat-heads on the wallpaper were opening and closing their mouths, as though sending silent cries.

Then Sabrina heard the sound. A low growl. She felt an icy wave of fear creep from her feet and create chilly butterflies in her stomach, as she sat up and fumbled for the bedside lamp switch. Light exploded and shattered the silver gloom, sent out a pink-tinted radiance that formed rough circle round the bed and was reflected in the wardrobe mirror.

The growl was repeated, only now it came from the region of the dressing-table. Sabrina strained her eyes, anxious to discover what caused this alarming noise, but at the same time terrified of what she might see. Suddenly she became aware of two little spots of yellow light that came round from behind the dressing-table and advanced into the room. Sabrina's hand flew to her mouth and she choked back a scream as an extremely large cat emerged into the circle of pink light. She had never seen such a cat before: long black fur that stood on end, ears laid back flat on either side of the round head, an open mouth that revealed long, pointed teeth, and eyes that glittered like polished amber discs. A long tail lashed from side to side.

The cat crept slowly forward, crouched low so that its stomach brushed the carpet. It stopped on reaching a position to the left of Sabrina's bed and looked up at her with hate-filled eyes. The growl rose to a terrifying howl.

From *The cat room* by R. Chetwynd-Hayes.

Put your stories into a class book so everyone in your class can read them. Decide on a title for the class book and design a cover for it.

Almost everyone has been scared at some time or another. When you go home, ask someone in your family about a scary experience they have had.
If possible, record the story on cassette. If not, write it down. Bring the story into school so other children can share it.

Fear of the dark

Read this poem by Paddy Kinsale, and then write down your answers to the questions about it:

Night shapes

Outside is full of cats and darkness,
Howling screeches and thick black stillness,
Things creeping silently,
Bats shuddering restlessly,
Owls hooting,
Moles rooting.

Outside is full of black shapes moving,
Shadows weird and slowly passing,
Things watching the dark,
Eyes looking for work,
Figures stealing,
Night brooding.

Outside is full of people dreaming,
Hoping, muttering, turning, scheming,
Ideas moving in the mind,
Voices uttering no sound
Time slipping
Dawn looming.

1 Why do you think the poet says "outside is full of cats"?

2 What things do you think will make "howling screech" noises in the dark?

3 List all the words which you think help this poem to sound spooky.

4 A lot of people, grown-ups as well as children, are afraid of the dark. Why do you think that is?

Draw or paint a picture of the Night Shapes.

Try and write a poem either about being frightened in the dark or about something or someone who frightens you. Make up a title for your poem.

Do you believe in ghosts?

A man named *Aidan Chambers* has written many books for children about ghosts and hauntings. Here, Mr Chambers tells the story of *The Headless Ghost* which was told to him by *Mr Fred Bayliss* who lived in Oxfordshire.

Well, it was roughly at the turn of the century that my father, courting my mother – my father living in Chipping Norton, and my mother at Milton-under-Wychwood – used to walk the six miles there and back, every Wednesday and Saturday, coming back early on Wednesday, but always leaving it till midnight on the Saturday. And just at the point of the road where he'd often heard what appeared to be a coach and horses go roaring across, through the Sarsden Pillars and on down through the drive, he always felt he'd like to come across a fellow traveller, especially on the dark nights.

And then, one night, he realized that he'd someone walking by the side of him, and being dark, he never bothered to look round, but started talking, and was quite happily talking away, never realizing that he was not actually getting any reply or conversation from the other person. And this happened on two dark nights.

And then the third night, when he was going along, it was almost full moon, and he never bothered to look round, as usual, and started talking, and then the fact that he wasn't getting any replies made him look round all of a sudden.

And what he had walking by the side of him was a headless Elizabethan gentleman, with his head tucked tightly under his arm. This, of course, thoroughly upset my father, and he took to his heels and fled, as far as Downs Hollow cottages, where he took refuge. And I'm afraid after that, my father changed the time he was walking along the road, and made quite sure he wasn't passing the Sarsden Pillars later than eleven o'clock at night. And that actually was the last time he saw the apparition.

Find out how many people in your class believe in ghosts. If anyone has had a ghostly experience, ask them to tell you about it.

Find out if your parents or grand-parents think they have ever seen a ghost. If they have, record their ghost story on cassette or take notes and then write it up when you are in school. Put the stories into your class book.

With two friends, imagine one of you is Mr Bayliss' father and the other people are newspaper reporters who've heard about the ghost. One reporter wants to believe Mr Bayliss but the other one thinks it's a silly story. Act out the interview. Afterwards, talk about how each of you felt when you were acting.
Did the person who played Mr Bayliss feel upset or angry when his story wasn't believed?
Did the reporter who didn't believe the story feel that he was right?

Now read this. It is a poem by W. S. Gilbert.

When the night wind howls in the chimney cowls, and
the bat in the moonlight flies,
And inky clouds, like funeral shrouds, sail over the
midnight skies –
When the footpads quail at the night-bird's wail, and
black dogs bay the moon,
Then is the spectres' holiday – then is the ghosts' high
noon!

As the sob of the breeze sweeps over the trees, and the
mists lie low on the fen,
From grey tombstones are gathered the bones that once
were women and men,
And away they go, with a mop and a mow, to the revel
that ends too soon,
For cockcrow limits our holiday – the dead of the night's
high noon!

And then each ghost with his ladye-toast to their church-
yard beds take flight,
With a kiss, perhaps, on her lantern chaps, and a grisly
grim "good night";
Till the welcome knell of the midnight bell rings forth its
jolliest tune,
And ushers our next high holiday – the dead of the night's
high noon!

Paint a picture of the ghost's high noon.

Now it's your turn!

Write a story or a poem for the people in your class about
ghosts, hauntings and things that go bump in the night.
Here are some things to choose from, but it's more fun to
make up your own.
The haunted house
Alone with a ghost
My friend, the ghost
In the cemetery
Remember to use frightening words in your story to
describe the ghost, and describe your feelings too.
Put your ghost story into your note book.

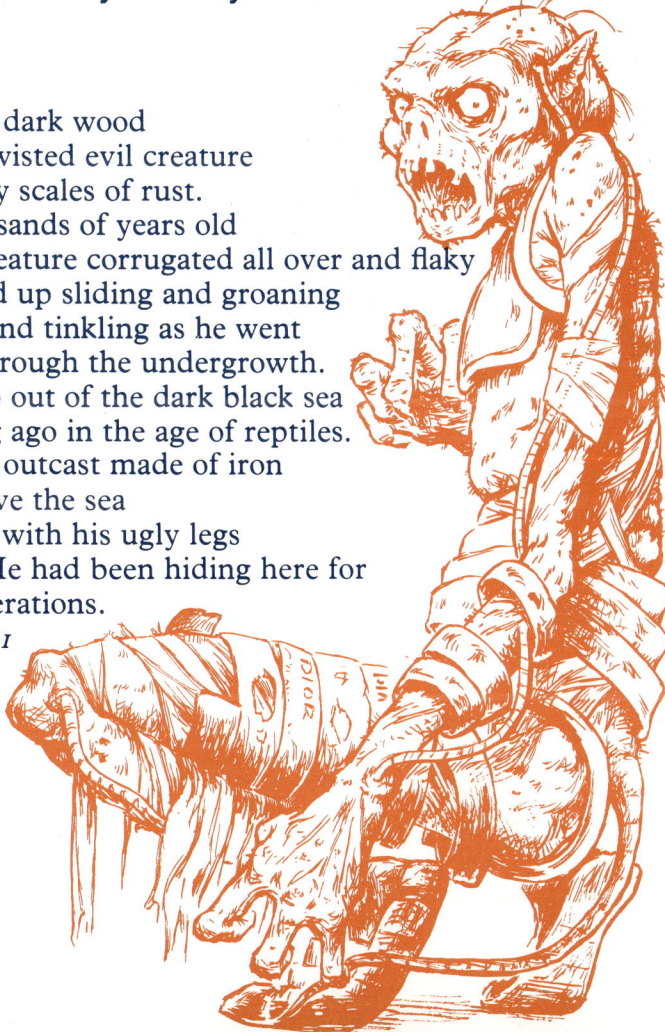

Fear of living things

People are often frightened of creatures like snakes, bats, spiders and even Alsatian dogs.
Here are some different poems about frightening creatures.
Read them all very carefully and then do the activities.

Out of the dark wood
Comes a twisted evil creature
Covered by scales of rust.
He is thousands of years old
An iron creature corrugated all over and flaky
He crawled up sliding and groaning
Clanking and tinkling as he went
Tearing through the undergrowth.
He rose up out of the dark black sea
Long, long ago in the age of reptiles.
He was an outcast made of iron
Had to leave the sea
And crawl with his ugly legs
On land. He had been hiding here for
Many generations.
Peter aged 11

Flies

Everywhere there are
Rotten, sickening, terrifying flies.
I get into bed to have a rest,
Well, I tried my best.
For all around were a
million
gillion
quartetzillion
Disgusting, annoying,
Awaking, destroying
Flies,
Flying around, over my cupboard and in my hair.

I itch, I twitch,
But I can't get them off.
I scratch, I kill,
But can't get them off.
I go to my bath
I drown them off, but not all.
I disinfect them;
I get my frog to eat them.
Sickening, horrifying, disgusting,
Those hairy, sucking, sucking, plague-bringers.
David Daniels aged 9

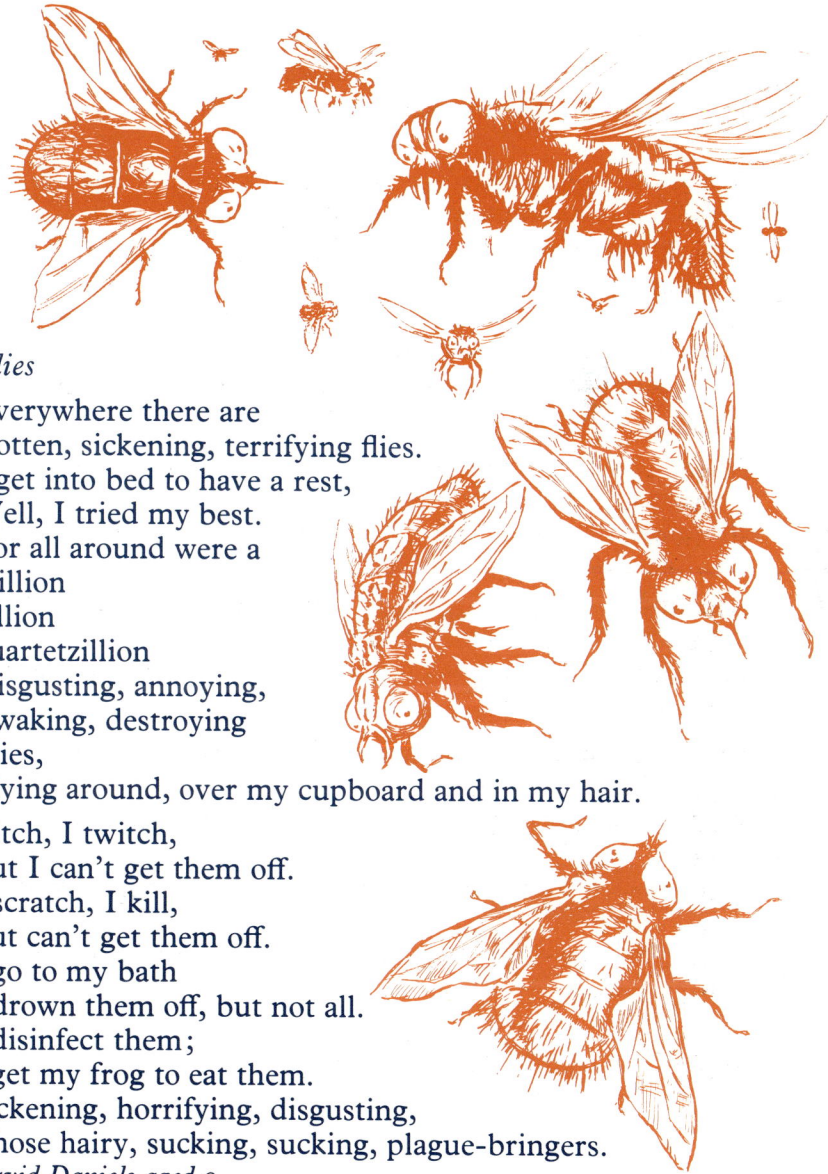

The Wendigo
The Wendigo!
Its eyes are ice and indigo!
Its blood is rank and yellowish!
Its voice is hoarse and bellowish!
Its tentacles are slithery,
And scummy,
Slimy,
Leathery!
Its lips are hungry blubbery,
And smacky,
Sucky,
Rubbery!
The Wendigo,
The Wendigo!
I saw it just a friend ago!
Last night it lurked in Canada;
Tonight, on your veranada!
As you are lolling hammockwise
It contemplates you stomachwise.
You loll,
It contemplates,
It lollops.
The rest is merely gulps and gollops.
Ogden Nash

1 Draw and colour pictures of each creature.
2 Make up a name for the creature in the first poem.
3 Which creature would you be most scared of, and why?
4 If there is a real creature which you are scared of write down its name and write about why you are frightened of it. Or write a poem.

Name calling

Sometimes children are scared or hurt when they are called names. Read what two children have to say:

I don't mind people called me names like Tarzan or Wurzal, but when people call me Chalky or something because I'm Chinese and make a face, it makes me very angry.

I don't mind being called funny names like Silver or money-bags because they are a bit like my real name. But I don't like being called Fatty. I think name calling is mean and spiteful.

Talk about your answers to these questions with your friends and teacher.

Are you ever called names?

How do you feel?

Do you ever call anybody else a name?

Why do you do it?

How do you think he or she feels?

A group of boys and girls made a list of names they felt people shouldn't use because the names are hurtful and rude.

spastic	fleabag	fatso
curry face	four eyes	nigger
wog	paki	cissy
tramp	coon	twiggy

With your teacher, talk about why you think these names could be hurtful.

Now carry out a survey in your class. Ask children to put down two names which they find very hurtful. Talk with your class about what you should do if you are called a name which you don't like.

Prejudice

Fear of the unknown or different can cause prejudice.

Look up the word prejudice in two dictionaries and find out what it means. Here is a simple definition to help you: *an unreasonable dislike of something or someone.* Write down your own meaning for prejudice.

Here are some reasons why children sometimes experience prejudice at school:

wearing glasses;
being a new boy or girl;
wearing different clothes;
having a different colour skin to most other children;
having a physical handicap;
being overweight or underweight;
having a different religion.

Choose two of the reasons and imagine that you are the person who is experiencing prejudice. Write a short story for each situation to explain what happens and how you feel. Discuss your stories with other children and compare them.

With one or two friends, make up a play based on one of your stories.

Here is a poem about prejudice.
What do you think the writer means when he says "you can't tell a book by its cover?"
Do you agree? Talk about this with your class and teacher.

Prejudice
Prejudice is just a thing
That you can't help.
People judge you by the colour of
   your skin
Or the clothes you wear.
But you can't tell a book by its cover.
Alton Scott

If prejudice is mainly based on fear and ignorance, how can we overcome it?
With your teacher, look at the eight possible reasons children sometimes experience prejudice. Discuss ways in which more knowledge and information would help you to overcome prejudice.
Can you think of any more reasons why people experience prejudice?

People talking

Have you ever really thought about how you talk?

– do you speak like the rest of your family?
– do you speak like your friends?
– do you ever change the way you talk depending on who you are talking to?
– how does the way you talk show your feelings?
– do you speak more than one language?

Make your own voice library

The best way to think about how you and other people talk, is to listen. To help you do this, you might like to make a cassette collection.

Working in 'twos', record people talking – in different places, at different times and doing different things. Put together all the cassettes which your class makes. Label and index the tapes so other people can use them. Wherever you see an asterisk like this *, you could add the work to your cassette collection.

As you work through this section, it would also really help if you could listen to the cassette which goes with this part of the book. Ask your teacher about it.

Changing the way we talk

People often change the way they talk depending on who they are talking to.

Here's what one boy from Yorkshire said about the way he talks, in and out of school.

"When relations come to our house, or when I'm in class at school I have to pronounce my words properly. But when I'm talking to my mates, I speak like they do. Like for 'water', I say 'watter', and for 'going', I say 'gooin'. We all talk in one general accent and we expect everybody else to talk like it. And if they don't – you know, if they talk too posh – then we think they're stuck up."

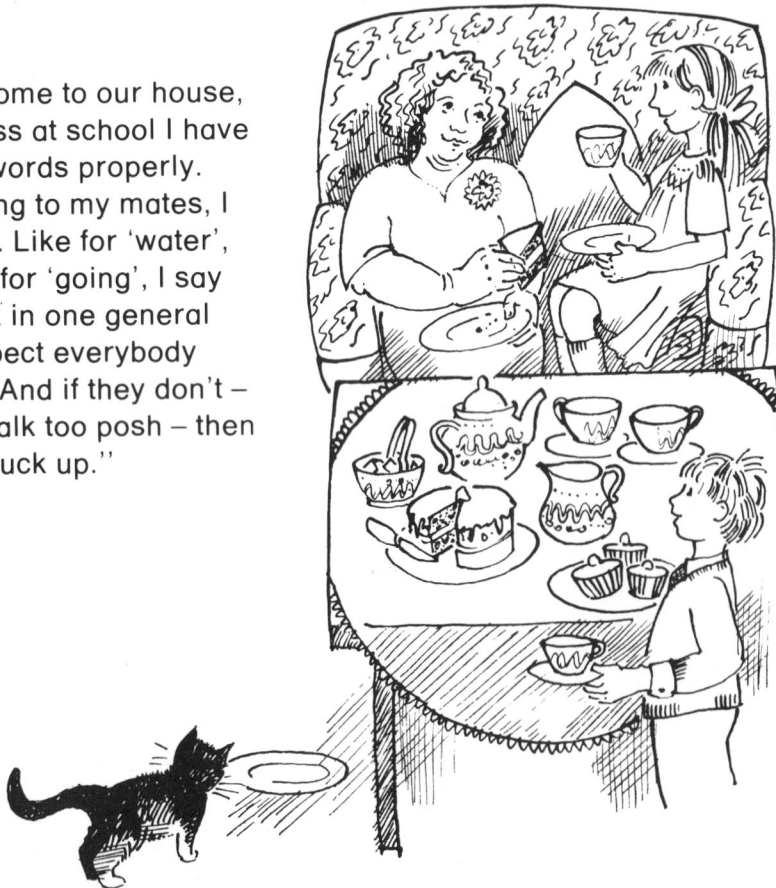

Now answer these questions:
1 Why does this boy think he has to pronounce his words in different ways when he's in class or when relations come to his house?
2 Why do you think he speaks like his mates when he's with them?
3 Why do you think the boy and his mates expect everybody else to talk like them?

Think of the different ways you speak when you are with your friends, when you are at home and when you are at school. **Talk about this with your friends and teacher.**

* Write down any words you would say differently, depending on who you are with (like the Yorkshire boy's "watter" and "water"). Record them on cassette.

Now read this. It is from a book called *One Small Boy* by Bill Naughton. Afterwards, write down your answers to the questions about it.

After three o'clock playtime on the Wednesday, Miss Skegham began a poetry lesson. The class was divided into four seasons, and each one had to chant a verse suitable to the season.

"Sheed, let me hear you give Spring," said Miss Skegham. "The rest of the class, silence."

Sheed faced her, giving a whisper first, "I'll spring you –," and then opening the right side of his mouth: "Summer is a-comin' in," he piped, "loudly sing cackoo."

"Cuckoo," she corrected.

"Cookoo, Cookoo," he trilled.

He admired the boy's coolness. If she asks me, he thought, I'll drop dead.

"M'Cloud," she called, "Let's hear 'The North Wind' from you."

He stood facing her and the circle of faces, his heart shaking, and praying mentally for help from the Virgin, he forced his dry voice out:

"The North wind doth blow,
And we shall have snow,
And what will the robin do then, poor ting?
He'll –"

"Ting?" she repeated. "Poor ting? Say 'thing'. Start from the beginning again. No need for you others to titter."

Ting, thing, ting, thing? He cleared his throat but couldn't remember the opening.

She said: "The North wind doth blow . . ." He coughed. The blood felt up to his eyes. Ting? thing? He'd have to watch for that.

"Right," she said.

He began: "The North wind doth blow. And we shall have snow, And what . . ."

"Not so fast," she said. "Go on. And what . . ."

"And what, and what will the robin do then . . ."

It was somewhere near and he'd have to watch out for it, they were all listening and watching him.

"Go on," she said. He went on: "And what will the robin do then, poor t-ting . . ."

"Ting! ting!" she said and he heard them all snigger. "Don't you know the King's English yet, M'Cloud?"

King's English – I'm Irish. She's saying that against the Irish. The flush died down and his face went cool.

"Thing!" she called out, "thing, thing, thing. Class, say 'poor thing'."

They let out one loud, "Poor thing".

"Right, M'Cloud," she said, in a rather kindly voice: "Yes, 'The North Wind . . .'." The nice touch in her voice almost startled him, but not quite. "M'Cloud," she shouted, "come on, 'The North Wind . . .'."

1 Why do you think McCloud pronounces "thing" as "ting"?

2 Why do you think the teacher wants him to pronounce it "thing"?

3 Has your teacher ever asked you to pronounce a word differently? What was the word?
How did you feel about being asked to pronounce it differently?

4 How do you think the boy feels when the teacher shouts at him about the way he talks?

5 What would you do if you were M'Cloud?
Either write a few short sentences or finish off the story in your own words.

Accents

Here's a story about a boy from the North of England, in which he tries to show how someone with a "posh" voice sounds to him.

Jim and I always take a short cut through some gardens when we're walking home. One day in this one garden there were lots of apples on the ground, and Jim picked one up and started to eat. All of a sudden, this woman came running out of the house and told us off. She said "Pat thet eppel down et once! This is praivat properteh. If I see you boys heah again ay will call the police!" Jim was so scared that he choked on the apple and could hardly run away.

Do you like some accents better than others?
Does your teacher?
Why do you think this is?
You might think it is because some accents are "better" or "more correct" than others. But they're not – they are all just different ways of talking which are as good as each other.

Read out loud the words which the woman says to Jim. Record them on cassette, then listen to them. How does your voice sound? Try saying other things in a "posh" voice. Try writing down what you say so other people will be able to read how it sounds (don't worry about spelling them properly).

Here's how a girl from Belfast in Northern Ireland wrote a poem so it would sound like the way she would say it. If you read it out loud, you should sound like you are from Belfast!
* Record yourself, if you like, to find out.

Ah wenna wahk
Up tu Sufeek
Tu c Jinny
Jinnys mah frenn.

Wuh luktd furer ma
Shuh wasna bout
So whu wen to the chippee
Tu ged som fussh
Wuh injoid id.
Kathleen Allen

If the poem was spelt in the ordinary way, it would look like this:

I went a walk
Up to Suffolk
To see Jenny
Jenny's my friend

We looked for her ma
She wasn't about
So we went to the chippy
To get some fish
We enjoyed it.

Try writing a story, a play or a poem so that when it is read out loud it will *sound* like you *talk*. Record your story so you can test what you have written.

The girl from Belfast who wrote the poem speaks with a Belfast accent. *Everybody speaks with some accent. Your accent depends on where you live, how your family talks and what kind of school you go to.*

There are many different accents in Britain. Even within Scotland or England, people's accents change a lot from one town to another. Most people on the television News speak with very similar accents, which may be different from yours. Watch some news programmes and notice what kind of accents the newsreaders and reporters have.

Here are two poems which have been written to sound like different accents. Next to each one you will see the same poem written with ordinary spellings. Try reading the two versions of each poem out loud.
How different do they sound?
If you have the cassette which goes with this book, you can listen to these poems on there, too.

Biby's Epitaph (a Cockney poem)
A muvver was barfin' 'er biby one night,
The youngest of ten and a tiny young mite,
The muvver was poor and the biby was thin,
Only a skelington covered in skin:
The muvver turned rahnd for the soap off
  the rack,
She was but a moment, but when she
  turned back,
The biby was gorn; and in anguish she cried,
"Oh, where is my biby?" – The angels
  replied:
"Your biby 'as fell dahn the plug-'ole,
Your biby 'as gorn dahn the plug;
The poor little thing was so skinny and thin
'E oughter been barfed in a jug;
Your biby is perfeckly 'appy,
'E won't need a barf any more,
Your biby 'as fell dahn the plug-'ole,
Not lorst, but gorn before."
Anon

Baby's Epitaph
A mother was bathing her baby one night,
The youngest of ten and a tiny young thing,
The mother was poor and the baby was thin,
Only a skeleton covered in skin:
The mother turned round for the soap off the rack,
She was but a moment, but when she turned back,
The baby was gone; and in anguish she cried,
"Oh, where is my baby?" – The angels replied:
"Your baby has fallen down the plug-hole,
Your baby has gone down the plug;
The poor little thing was so skinny and thin
He should have been bathed in a jug;
Your baby is perfectly happy,
He won't need a bath any more,
Your baby has fallen down the plug-hole,
Not lost, but gone before."

Six O'Clock News (a Glasgow poem)

this is thi	this is the
six a clock	six o'clock
news thi	news the
man said n	man said and
thi reason	the reason
a talk wia	I talk with a
BBC accent	BBC accent
iz coz yi	is because you
widny wahnt	wouldn't want
mi ti talk	me to talk
aboot thi	about the
trooth wia	truth with
voice lik	a voice like
wanna yoo	one of you
scruff. if	scruffs. if
a toktaboot	I talked about
thi trooth	the truth
lik wanna yoo	like one of you
scruff yi	scruffs you
widny thingk	wouldn't think
it wuz troo.	it was true.
jist wanna yoo	just one of your
scruff tokn.	scruffs talking.
thirza right	there's a right
way ti spell	way to spell
ana right way	and a right way
ti tok it. this	to talk. this is
is me tokn yir	me talking your
right way a	right way of
spellin. this	spelling. this
is ma trooth.	is my truth.
yooz doant no	you don't know
thi trooth	the truth
yirsellz cawz	yourselves because
yi canny talk	you can't talk
right. this is	right. this is
the six a clock	the six o'clock
nyooz. belt up.	news. belt up.

Tom Leonard

*Choose one of the poems and record yourself saying it in your own way – with your own accent.

22

Dialects

As well as speaking with different accents, people in different parts of Britain sometimes also use different words. These different words are part of their local dialect. Everybody speaks in a dialect of some kind. The dialect used by most readers on TV and in books and newspapers is called **Standard English.**

People's dialects in different parts of the country tell you something about history.

Cockney rhyming slang

Over a hundred years ago in London, people began to speak in what is called "rhyming slang". Instead of saying a word, they would say one which rhymed with it like this:

Trouble and strife – *the wife*
Plates of meat – *feet*
Dustbin lids – *kids*
Boat race – *face*
Loaf of bread – *head*
North and south – *mouth*
Rosy lea – *tea*

Scouse dialect

Scouse was originally the name of a stew made from the cheapest cuts of meat, boiled with onions and potatoes. Somehow this became the name for the dialect that people from Liverpool speak!

Here are some useful words and phrases to help you speak Liverpool dialect with a Liverpool accent.

Scouse	Standard English
Ullo dur	Hello there
Ta wack	Thank you
I don know a blind were e says.	I don't understand him.
Worrell	What will
Darrell	That will
Dale	They will
Give yer chin a rest	Please be quiet
Gear	Excellent, good
Ee's a good skin	I like him
Yer gorra cob on	You are in a bad mood
Are moggy	Our cat
Ee's a mush	He's a stranger
Bone orchard	A cemetery
Ave yer gorrany?	Have you got any . . .?
I'm saggin skewl	I'm playing truant
Ee wuz wellied	He was kicked
De scuffer	A policeman
De judy scuffer	A policewoman
Kecks	Trousers
Purra desert wellies	A pair of sandals

Frank Shaw

Things to do with a friend

1 Make up your own rhyming slang. It could become your own secret language.

2 Make a dialect dictionary. Write down the words and phrases that you and your friends use and translate them into Standard English dialect. Remember to organise your dictionary alphabetically so you can easily look up words.

3 If you live in an area where there is a strong local dialect, make a note book of dialect words and phrases. Use a cassette recorder to tape examples of people speaking in your local dialect. Older people might remember more dialect words than younger ones. Listen to the dialect and then try to write it out in Standard English.

Do you think Standard English is a more correct way of talking than your local dialect? Discuss this with your class and teacher. Does your teacher ever ask you not to speak in your local dialect?
How do you feel?

This is an extract from a poem called *Bans O'Killing* by a Jamaican woman, Louise Bennett.
She is angry that Jamaican dialect is criticised just because English people speak in a different way. "How is Jamaican any different from Yorkshire, Cockney or Irish?" she asks.

You can listen to the poem on the cassette which goes with this book.

West Indian dialects are interesting because they have some words which seem to come from the African languages spoken by the ancestors of West Indians.
Does anybody in your class (or someone in your family) speak a dialect of English from another country like
– West Indian English?
– American English?
– Australian English?

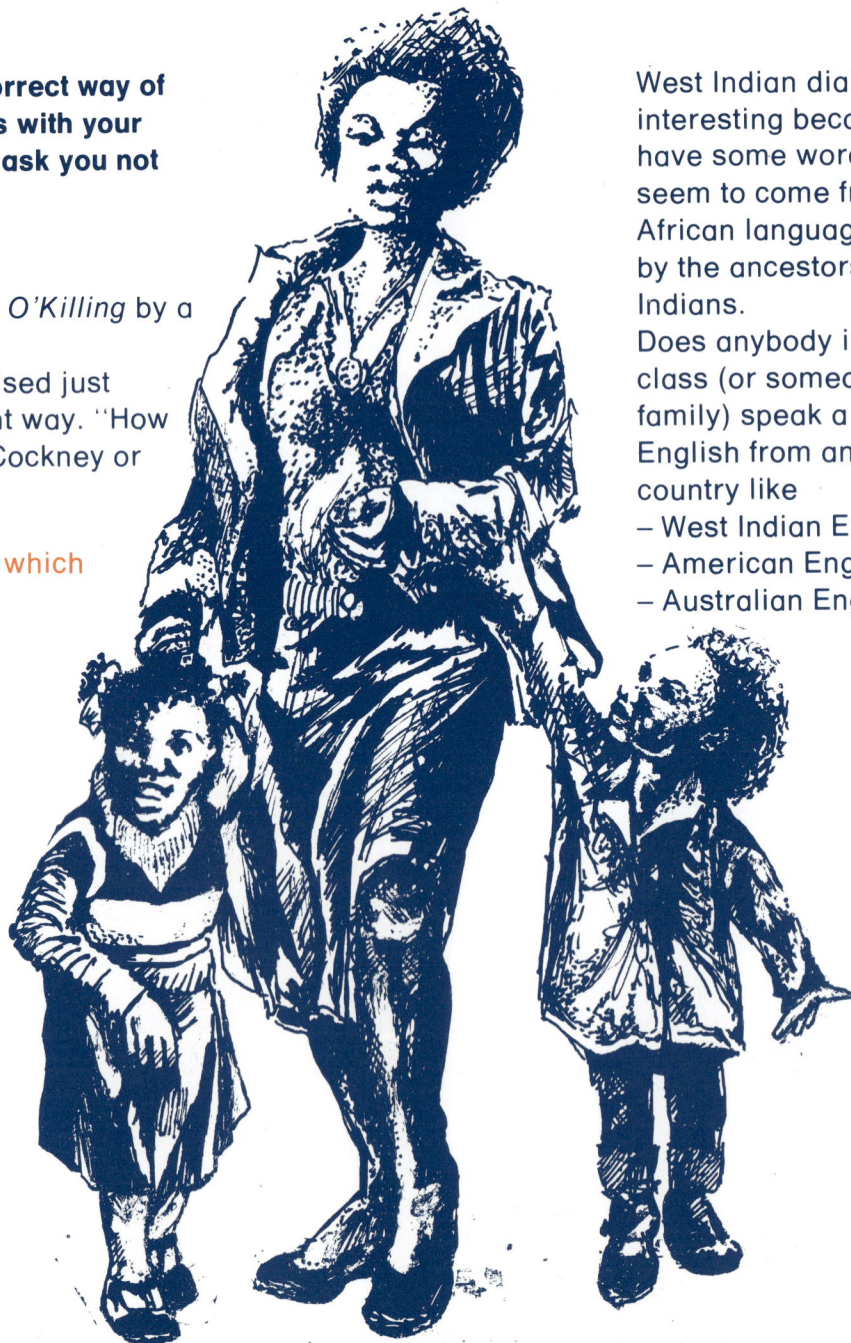

Dah language wey yuh proud o'
Weh yuh honour and respeck
Po' Mass Charlie! Yuh noh know sey
Dat it spring from dialect!

Dat dem start fe try tun language
From de fourteen century
Five hundred years gawn an dem got
More dialect dan we!

Yuyh wi haffe kill de Lancashire
De Yorkshire, de Cockney
De broad Scotch an de Irish brogue
Before yuh start kill me!

Yuh wi haffe get de Oxford book
O' English verse, an tear
Out Chaucer, Burns, Lady Grizelle
An plenty o' Shakespeare!

Speaking two languages

**Do you speak another language?
Does anyone in your family or in
your class speak another
language?**

Find someone who speaks another
language that you don't know and
ask him to tell you the words in his
language for
*Hello
How are you?
What time is it?
I am very well
Goodbye*

If you do speak two languages, you
are very lucky to have learnt to do
this when you were young (it gets
harder as you grow up).

**Did anyone in your family grow up
in another country?**
If so you could ask them to come
into school and tell the class what it
is like to be a child in another
country. (But ask your teacher if this
will be all right, first.)

Stornoway
Gaelic
Punjabi

GAELIC

Glasgow
Gaelic Punjabi Urdu
Polish Italian
Cantonese

Leicester
Gujerati Punjabi
Polish

Bradford
Punjabi Polish
Urdu Ukranian
Gujerati

Coventry
Polish Punjabi
Gujerati Cantonese

Peterborough
Punjabi Italian
Polish Gujerati
Cantonese

Liverpool
Cantonese Welsh
Punjabi Gujerati

Birmingham
Punjabi Turkish
Gujerati Bengali Urdu
Arabic Spanish
Greek

WELSH

Bedford
Italian Punjabi

London
Greek Turkish Bengali
Spanish Gujerati Italian
Punjabi Urdu Cantonese
Portuguese Arabic Hindi

Cardiff
Gujerati Cantonese
Urdu Welsh

This map shows you two things:
1 Some of the other languages which are spoken in Britain;
2 Some of the places where the people live who speak these languages.
You can copy this map if you want to.

Showing how we feel

How many ways can you say the same thing?

Here's one way to find out! You will need a cassette recorder and one friend to help you.

Read this telephone conversation:

First speaker	Second speaker
Hello	Hello
How are you?	O.K.
We've just come back from holiday.	Oh, really?
Peter fell over the cliff.	Oh
He broke his leg.	How horrible for him.
It was terrible!	What a shame!

Look again at the words the second speaker says. Practice saying them so you sound *surprised* to hear what the first speaker has said. They say them again so you sound *bored*. Then say them again so you sound *amused*.

Now record the conversation on tape, with you and your friend acting the parts of the speakers. Do it three times and each time the second speaker should sound different – surprised, bored and amused.

Listen to the tape. Has the sound of the second speaker's voice shown how your friend feels?

Try making up some more conversations on tape. Play them to some other friends and see if they can tell how you were feeling by the sound of your voice. Record a conversation where one of you tries to sound as though your feelings are changing as the conversation goes along.

Listen to the cassette tape which goes with this book. There are more examples of this on there.

The things people say

Do some things which people say get on your nerves?
Read this by Elaine Slater. It is called *No Buts.*

"But Dad"
"No buts Andy you're going if you like it or not",
"But . . ."
"Look you're coming and that's that!"
"But I've got my homework to do . . ."
"You can do that when you get home!"
"But Dad!"
"No buts son you're coming no matter what you say"
"Oh all right dad"
"That's better son"

Now it's your turn!

Think of five things people say to you which get on your nerves. With two friends, write down a list. Over the next three days, notice how often you hear anybody saying these things. Score one point every time somebody says one of these sayings on your list. After the three days are over, see which saying has the most points.

Here are five sayings which some children said got on their nerves:
B.E.D. spells bed.
I haven't the time for that now.
You stupid child!
Watch it, four eyes.
This will end in tears, I'm warning you.

You should now have a class cassette collection – recordings of dialects and accents, recordings of yourself and your friends and recordings of local people talking. Don't forget to label and index your collection carefully so you and other people can use it. If you or your teacher has friends in another part of the country, you could exchange cassettes so you can listen to the accents and dialects they have collected.

Sadness and happiness

In this section you will explore the feelings of sadness and happiness. First you will need a book or folder to put all your different pieces of work into. Then you will need to prepare the front cover and give your book a title.

Home school interviews

When you go home, tell your family about this section of the book and see if they will help you. Interview as many relations as you can and ask them to tell you about two sad times and two happy times they can remember. Record them on cassette ready to write up at school or take notes and write those up at school. Put your writing into your book. If they aren't too personal, they will be interesting for other children to read.

"A time to weep and a time to laugh"

What things make you laugh?
When do you cry?
What is happiness?
What is sadness?

In your book, make a list of all the things which make you happy and those which make you sad.
Here is how one boy wrote out his list:

> 1) Sadness is when I have to wait for my mum to get up to give me my breakfast.
> 2) Sadness is when I have to go to bed early on a Sunday.
> 3) Sadness is when my mum's friend dies.
> 4) Sadness is when I am ill and I can't go to the school outing.
> 5) Happiness is when I go to the seaside.
> 6) Happiness is when I go home to Barbados.
> 7) Happiness is when me and Paul Parkin go to Miss' house.
> 8) Happiness is watching Albert Costello films.
> 9) Happiness is when we win the football cup.

Ask other children what makes them sad and happy. Write down what they tell you in your book.

Make them laugh!

Making people laugh is often a good way to help people forget they are sad – even if only for a short time. Somebody else's bad luck often makes us laugh, too. Here is an examples from a book called *The book of heroic failures*.

The Most Unsuccessful Prison Escape
After weeks of extremely careful planning, seventy-five convicts completely failed to escape from Saltillo Prison in Northern Mexico. In November 1975 they had started digging a secret tunnel designed to bring them up at the other side of the prison wall.

On 18 April 1976, guided by pure genius, their tunnel came up in the nearby courtroom in which many of them had been sentenced. The surprised judges returned all 75 to jail.

If you have your own disaster story (which is really rather funny!), write it out in your book.

Times of sadness

Pets matter very much to many children and they feel deeply about them.
Read this poem carefully and quietly. It is a sad poem.

Death of a cat

I rose early
On the fourth day
Of his illness,
And went downstairs
To see if he was
All right.

He was not in the
House, and I rushed
Wildly round the
Garden calling his name.

I found him lying
Under a rhododendron
Bush,
His black fur
Wet, and matted
With the dew.

I knelt down beside him.
And he opened his
Mouth as if to
Miaow
But no sound came.

I picked him up
And he lay quietly
In my arms
As I carried him
Indoors.

Suddenly he gave
A quiet miaow
And I felt his body tense,
And then lie still.
Anthony Thompson

Work with two other children who have read the poem.
Discuss it with them. How did you all feel when you read the poem?
Would you have picked up the cat from under the rhododendron bush? Why did the cat go there?
How did you feel when you read the poem?

Now read this next poem (together). How is it different from the first one?

Rock, our dog

He's dead now.
He was put to sleep last night.
I was sad,
But I did not cry.

It was not the same
Without him here
To prance and
Nuzzle his head
Into my arms.

Today we are going
To bury him
In the garden
I helped dig the hole,
And then ran off.
Nicholas Hadfield

Talk about these questions too:
Do you think that the boy misses his dog?
How was the death of Rock different to the death of the cat? Why do you think the boy ran off after the hole had been dug?

Sometimes poems are the best way to express feelings – much better than just writing a straightforward account of the facts like you might read in a newspaper.

Now read this poem and then discuss it with your two friends.
What do you all think of the poem?
How did you *feel* when you read it?

Poem

I wish this poem
was an arm around you
which could
comfort you.

I wish this poem
was a room,
with a glowing fire in it
so that you could curl yourself up.

I wish that this
was so much more
for you.

I wish you would
wish on this poem. And then, maybe,
you wouldn't cry.
Henryk Borowski

What situations can you all think of when someone would be happy to receive this poem?

Now it's your turn!

Either by yourself or with your friends, try to write a poem about a very sad or happy time you can remember. Read your poem to your friends or even the whole class. Put it into your book.

Now read this poem:

The Burial

As the clock struck one
The old man died.
He lay there,
Still,
Cold,
And white.
His wrinkled old face
And his still clear eyes,
No longer to see the world outside.

Then they gently placed him
In his own small coffin
Of white satin
And of silk,
With large brass handles.
And then they nailed him in.

The black hearse arrived
And the doors were opened.
Then four men
Dressed in black
Carried the coffin to the car,
And gently slid it in,
With the beautiful wreaths
Of carnations and roses
Placed on the top.
The hearse
Slowly
Moved.

Down the so familiar streets
Where he had so often walked
On summer days
And winter nights.
To end like this
In a big black hearse.

People stared
As they neared the church,
Wondering who had died.
Then the hearse stopped
Before the graveyard gates
And once again
He was carried upon high.

The hymns were sung,
And the prayers were said,
And they carried him outside
To a deep,
Dark, hole.
And gently they lowered him
Down,
And down.
Until at last
It came to rest
upon the hard black earth.

The blessing was said
As the priest
Sprinkled earth into the grave.
And as the people sobbed
And moved away
The grave was slowly filled.

And then the wreaths
Of beautiful flowers
Were placed upon the top
Until they perished,
And were thrown away.
Pauline Norrie

Discuss your answers to these questions with your friends:
1 Each line of the poem is quite short. How do you think that helps the writer to express herself?
2 Does the writer tell you her own feelings about the burial?
3 Do you think the writer had actually seen a burial or did she just imagine it?

By yourself, take out all the information from the poem (scribble down notes on scrap paper) and use the information to re-write the poem as a straightforward factual account of the burial.
How does it compare with the poem? Discuss your account and compare with the other children's in your discussion group.

The funeral in this poem was a traditional British one with a church service. People celebrate death in different ways all over the world as well as in Britain. In some countries, death is a joyous occasion. If you have ever been to a funeral, maybe it was different from the one in this poem. Perhaps you would like to talk about it with your group.

Discussion
People are often reluctant to talk about death (or bereavement, as it is sometimes called). Losing someone who is close to us is perhaps the hardest thing any of us have to bear. Do you think it would help if we could talk about it more? Or do you think it is far too personal and private an experience to discuss?
Discuss this in your group.
Would you agree with the saying, "A problem shared is a problem halved"?

From sadness to joy!

Some stories start with a sad beginning and have a happy ending. Others do the reverse. Collect some fairy tales by *Hans Anderson* or the *Brothers Grimm*. Choose six stories you like and see which pattern they follow. Write down what happens at the beginning and the end.

Here is the beginning of a story by Oscar Wilde called The Selfish Giant. It begins with a very sad situation. Read the extract carefully and then work out how to continue and complete the story in your own words. (Remember to think about for what age children you are writing.) Did you give your story a sad or happy ending? When you have written your version, and your teacher has checked it, find some children to read it to.

Every afternoon, as they were coming from school, the children used to go and play in the Giant's garden.

It was a large lovely garden, with soft green grass. Here and there over the grass stood beautiful flowers like stars, and there were twelve peach-trees that in the spring-time broke out into delicate blossoms of pink and pearl, and in the autumn bore rich fruit. The birds sat on the trees and sang so sweetly that the children used to stop their games in order to listen to them. "How happy we are here!" they cried to each other.

One day the Giant came back. He had been to visit his friend the Cornish ogre, and had stayed with him for seven years. After the seven years were over he had said all that he had to say, for his conversation was limited, and he determined to return to his own castle. When he arrived he saw the children playing in the garden.

"What are you doing here?" he cried in a very gruff voice, and the children ran away.

"My own garden is my own garden," said the Giant; "anyone can understand that, and I will allow nobody to play in it but myself." So he built a high wall all round it, and put up a notice-board.

TRESPASSERS
WILL BE
PROSECUTED

He was a very selfish Giant.
The poor children had now nowhere to play.

Perhaps you may like to read the original version to see how Oscar Wilde really finished the story!

Now read this. It is an extract from a book called *The trouble with Donovan Croft* by Bernard Ashley. Donovan is a West Indian boy who is fostered by a white family. Donovan misses his home and his parents. In fact, he is so sad that he can't bring himself to speak. Everyone at school makes fun of him.

The moist channels of undried tears on Donovan's cheeks were swelled by two large tear-drops. Welling up from the sad depths of his eyes they trickled down to his jaw and wet the front of his tee-shirt. He sat on a wooden box in the dusty corner and smelt the sweet aroma of cut cedar.

In his utter misery he thought about home. He had had a home until yesterday. Even though his mother had left them a few weeks ago he had still had a home. It had been a sad home, and lonely when his mother had gone, and life seemed to have come to a stop that day he had woken up to a breakfast prepared by his father; but he had still had a place to come back to, and a father to cry to, and to see crying. Now his father had sent him away, and there was nothing left of the happy days. He was alone and unwanted, and while he cried out for his parents' love again, he felt betrayed by the people he most wanted.

"Where you gone, Mam? Why you gone away? I love you and you go away. And I feel bad. I feel real bad."

Donovan's thoughts were unspoken, but all the same they were meant to be heard, even if the tiny creature he was holding in his cupped hands could not understand them. The little face looked up at him but Donovan did not see it. In the misty, unfocused eye of his mind there was only the picture of his mother, a slim, pretty woman who smiled and loved and drew out from Donovan a love that he could feel. For some white boys, living in a neighbourhood where their parents had grown up, a prominent memory of their mothers might have been of a time when they were comforted over a cut knee or a bruised head. But for Donovan such memories were of times when he had been wounded by words rather than by stones.

"You always love me. You always kiss me and love me. When the boys call me names and I cry you say, 'Never mind, boy, we are all the same, and we are all together: your daddy loves you and your mammy loves you: we are all together, and let them call you any old thing.' Then I don't cry any more."

The story does have a happy ending but to find out what it is, you'll have to read the book yourself!

With three friends, discuss what you all think Donovan needs most.

Times of happiness

Scrooge is a miserable character in Charles Dickens' book, *A Christmas Carol*. He is mean and bad tempered. Bob Cratchit is Scrooge's underpaid clerk who has a crippled child called Tiny Tim. Bob's family, like many people in Victorian times, was very, very poor. Even so, Christmas was always a time of great celebration and happiness. Here is part of the description of Christmas dinner at the Cratchit's.

There was never such a goose. Bob said he didn't believe there ever was such a goose cooked. Its tenderness and flavour, size and cheapness, were the themes of universal admiration. Eked out by apple-sauce and mashed potatoes, it was a sufficient dinner for the whole family; indeed, as Mrs Cratchit said with great delight (surveying one small atom of bone upon the dish), they hadn't ate it all at last! Yet every one had had enough, and the youngest Cratchits in particular, were steeped in sage and onion to the eyebrows! But now, the plates being changed by Miss Belinda, Mrs Cratchit left the room alone – too nervous to bear witnesses – to take the pudding up and bring it in.

Suppose it should not be done enough! Suppose it should break in turning out! Suppose somebody should have got over the wall of the back-yard, and stolen it, while they were merry with the goose – a supposition at which the two young Cratchits became livid! All sorts of horrors were supposed.

Hallo! A great deal of steam! The pudding was out of the copper. A smell like a washing-day! That was the cloth. A smell like an eating-house and a pastrycook's next door to each other, with a laundress's next door to that! That was the pudding! In half a minute Mrs Cratchit entered – flushed, but smiling proudly – with the pudding, like a speckled cannon-ball, so hard and firm, blazing in half of half-a-quartern of ignited brandy, and bedight with Christmas holly stuck into the top.

"Oh, a wonderful pudding!" Bob Cratchit said, and calmly too, that he regarded it as the greatest success achieved by Mrs Cratchit since their marriage. Mrs Cratchit said that now the weight was off her mind, she would confess she had had her doubts about the quantity of flour. Everybody had something to say about it, but nobody said or thought it was at all a small pudding for a large family. It would have been flat heresy to do so. Any Cratchit would have blushed to hint at such a thing.

At last the dinner was all done, the cloth was cleared, the hearth swept, and the fire made up. The compound in the jug being tasted,

and considered perfect, apples and oranges were put upon the table, and a shovel-full of chestnuts on the fire. Then all the Cratchit family drew round the hearth, in what Bob Cratchit called a circle, meaning half a one; and at Bob Cratchit's elbow stood the family display of glass. Two tumblers, and a custard-cup without a handle.

These held the hot stuff from the jug, however, as well as golden goblets would have done; and Bob served it out with beaming looks, while the chestnuts on the fire sputtered and cracked noisily. Then Bob proposed:

"A Merry Christmas to us all, my dears. God bless us!"

Which all the family re-echoed.

"God bless us every one!" said Tiny Tim, the last of all.

Things to do

1 Are there any words you don't understand? Using a dictionary, check the meanings of any words you may not be sure of.
2 There is just one point in this extract where you might realise the family are very poor.
What does Dickens say?
3 Which words, phrases or expressions indicate that the story is about people living in the nineteenth century?
4 What is it in the story which gives such a feeling of joy?
Talk about your answers to the last three questions with your class and teacher.

Write a story

About a really happy celebration or occasion in your life. Just like Dickens did, write your story so that the reader will be able to feel how happy you were.

Without words

Just imagine what it would be like to arrive on an island where no-one had ever been before.

Perhaps you have been shipwrecked and washed up on the shore of a strange land. You walk off the beach and find a village. People come out of their houses and seem friendly. But you cannot speak their language and you can't understand what they are saying to you. The villagers will want to know who you are and where you have come from. You probably need to ask for some food and to find out where you are. What can you do?

Act it out

Working with a friend, pretend that one of you is the castaway and the other a villager. Try to find out all about each other without using any words at all.

The castaway

You must try to:
– explain where you are from and how you arrived on the island;
– ask for food and anything else you need;
– find out where you are. Is there a big city or town nearby and, if so, can you get there?
– find out who the people in the village are;
– find out the name of the villager to whom you are talking and anything else you want to know about him or her.

The villager

You must try to
– find out who the castaway is and where he or she is from;
– find out if he or she needs any help;
– tell him or her some useful things about the country you live in (perhaps there are fierce animals or poisonous snakes);
– direct him or her to the nearest big town or city.

Acting this out probably made you realise how useful words are and how difficult life would be without them! But you also probably found out that you could communicate reasonably well by making signs, pulling faces and pointing at things. All these ways of communicating are called **gestures.**

Now read this:

It is an extract from a book called *Stig of the dump* by Clive King. The book is about a boy called Barney and his strange friend called Stig. In this extract, Barney has fallen into a pit and meets Stig for the first time.

He'd never seen anything like the collection of bits and pieces, odds and ends, bric-a-brac and old brock, that this Stig creature had lying about his den. There were stones and bones, fossils and bottles, skins and tins, stacks of sticks and hanks of string. There were motor-car tyres and hats from old scarecrows, nuts and bolts and bobbles from brass bedsteads. There was a coal scuttle full of dead electric light bulbs and a basin with rusty screws and nails in it. There was a pile of bracken and newspapers that looked as if it were used for a bed. The place looked as if it had never been given a tidy-up.

"I wish I lived here," said Barney.

Stig seemed to understand that Barney was approving of his home and his face lit up. He took on the air of a householder showing a visitor round his property, and began pointing out some of the things he seemed particularly proud of.

First, the plumbing. Where the water dripped through a crack in the roof of the cave he had wedged the mud-guard of a bicycle. The water ran along this, through the tube of a vacuum-cleaner, and into a big can with writing on it. By the side of this was a plastic football cut in half, and Stig dipped up some water and offered it to Barney. Barney had swallowed a mouthful before he made out the writing on the can: it said WEEDKILLER However, the water only tasted of rust and rubber.

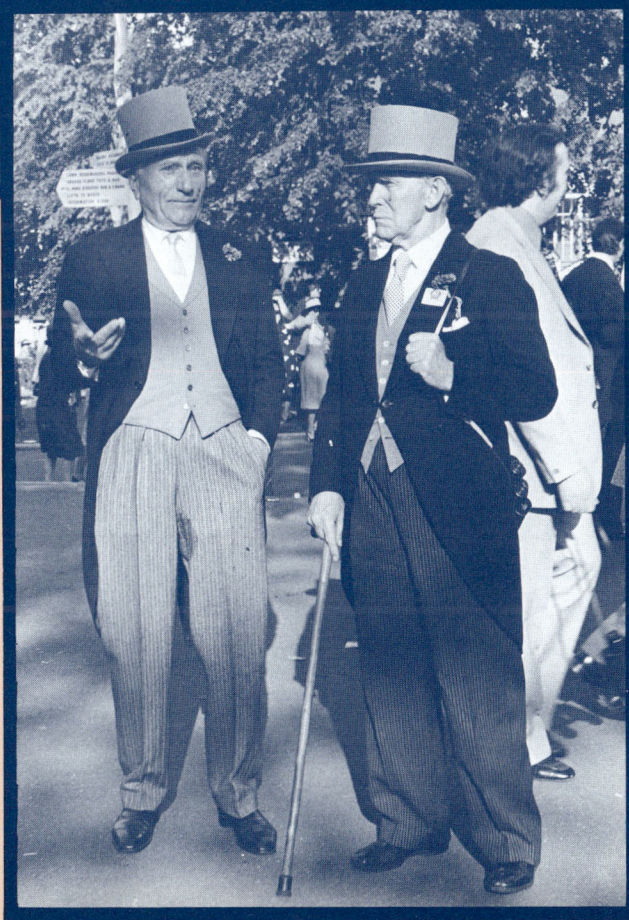

**Now look at these three photographs
and for each one write down**
- what kind of people you think they
  are;
- how old they are;
- what they are doing;
- how they feel.

Compare what you have written
with what one of your friends has
written. Then think of three
questions you would like to ask the
people in the photographs to find
out if your first impressions of them
are right.

How well can you show your feelings without using words?

In a group of three, take it
in turns to each mime one
of the following situations.
You must express your
feelings without using
words.
1 Biting a rotten apple
and feeling sick.
2 Being scared in a
haunted house.
3 Pricking your finger
with a safety pin.

Can your friends guess
what you are feeling?

45

A picture is worth a thousand words

Do you agree with this statement?

Look carefully at this painting to help you make up your mind.

Now write down your answers to these questions:

1 How do you think the people in the painting are related to one another?
2 Take each face in turn and describe its expression.
3 What can you find out from looking carefully at the man's clothes?
4 Now look at the hands in the painting. What do they tell you about the people?

There are many possible interpretations of the story behind this painting. Write an account of your version of the story, using about 100 words. Compare your version with a friend's.

Now look at the bottom of this page to find out more about the painting.

The painting is called On Strike *and was painted by Hubert Herkomer in 1891. The workman is angry and bitter because he has had to go on strike to improve his working conditions. His wife is sorrowful because the strike means they are going to be short of money.*

Symbols

Another way people can exchange information without using words is by using symbols to represent things. Symbols are used on maps.

Here are some symbols used on ordnance survey maps of Britain:

a bus station

a church with a tower

a church with a spire

a working windmill

a disused windmill

a youth hostel

Now make up good map symbols for a zoo, a car park and a supermarket. (Perhaps your teacher could find you a real ordnance survey map.)

With a friend, draw a map of the area around your school. Use ordnance survey symbols to show where things like churches and bus stations are and use any of your own symbols to show other important or useful buildings. Put a key at the bottom of your map (a key is a list of all the symbols you have used and an explanation of what each one means).

Make up some good symbols for road signs to tell people that there is
– a swimming pool
– a library
– a museum nearby.

There are also symbols on some road signs and at railway stations. These symbols often tell people that different services are available. You will probably have seen these symbols on road signs:

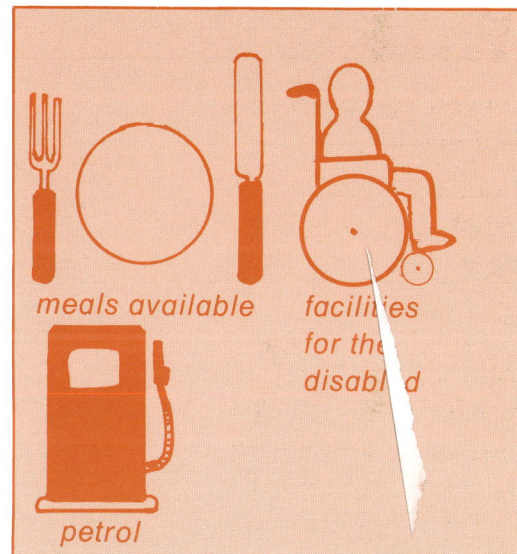

meals available

facilities for the disabled

petrol

Signs like these are used much more since Britain joined the Common Market. All over Europe, the same symbols are used on signs. This helps everyone to understand the signs even though they may speak different languages.

Outer space

It is the year 2010 AD. The Earth has drifted towards the sun and is beginning to burn. Poisonous gas fills the Earth's atmosphere.
Earth must be evacuated!

When you go home, ask your family how they would feel if they found out the Earth was to be evacuated. What major problems are there on Earth at present which they would like to see solved on a new planet?
Discuss this with your class and teacher.

Imagine you and your friends are on Earth in the year 2010 AD. Talk about how you would feel once you knew Earth had to be evacuated.
What would you want to do and who would you want to see before you left your planet?

Write a diary for your last week on Earth.

Various plans have been made to accommodate the Earth's population. Some people will be shuttled to stations in outer space and others will be re-settled on new planets further from the sun.

You and your friends are being re-settled on the planet **Theta** which is at the edge of our galaxy. It will take 200 days to travel there. Theta is much colder than Earth and only has four hours of dim sunlight each day. But you can drink the water, breathe the air and the gravity is the same as Earth's.
First of all, you must fill in a data sheet like this for Earth control:

Name _____
Age _____
Date of birth _____
Last address _____
on earth _____

Height _____ Weight _____
Hair colour _____
Colour of eyes _____

Personal Data Sheet

Put your data sheet into a folder and mark your folder *Earth 3000 – Theta*. **You must have this folder with you at all times and keep all the work you do inside it.**

Personal choice

Each evacuee from Earth can take three objects with him (no bigger than a cornflakes packet). Think about which three objects you would choose and then list them on a piece of paper. Write down the reasons for your choice.
Keep the paper in your folder. You may need it later!
Draw or paint the objects for your folder.
Talk about your choice with your friends and teacher.

Because you will be in space for 200 days, you will travel on a highly-developed sky-lab rocket. This contains all the life support systems needed for the journey, for up to four people.

Here is a drawing of your rocket. The solar panels provide power for all the instruments inside the space craft.

Decide which three people are going to travel with you in sky-lab. The four of you will form a **command group.** Choose a name for your group and make sure you each write it on your folders.

Remember! The four of you will have to live and work together for a long time. Make a list of the qualities of each person and explain why you think you have a balanced team in your command group. Look carefully at your friends' strengths and weaknesses as well as your own.

Discuss your choice of people with your teacher. Put your list into your folder.

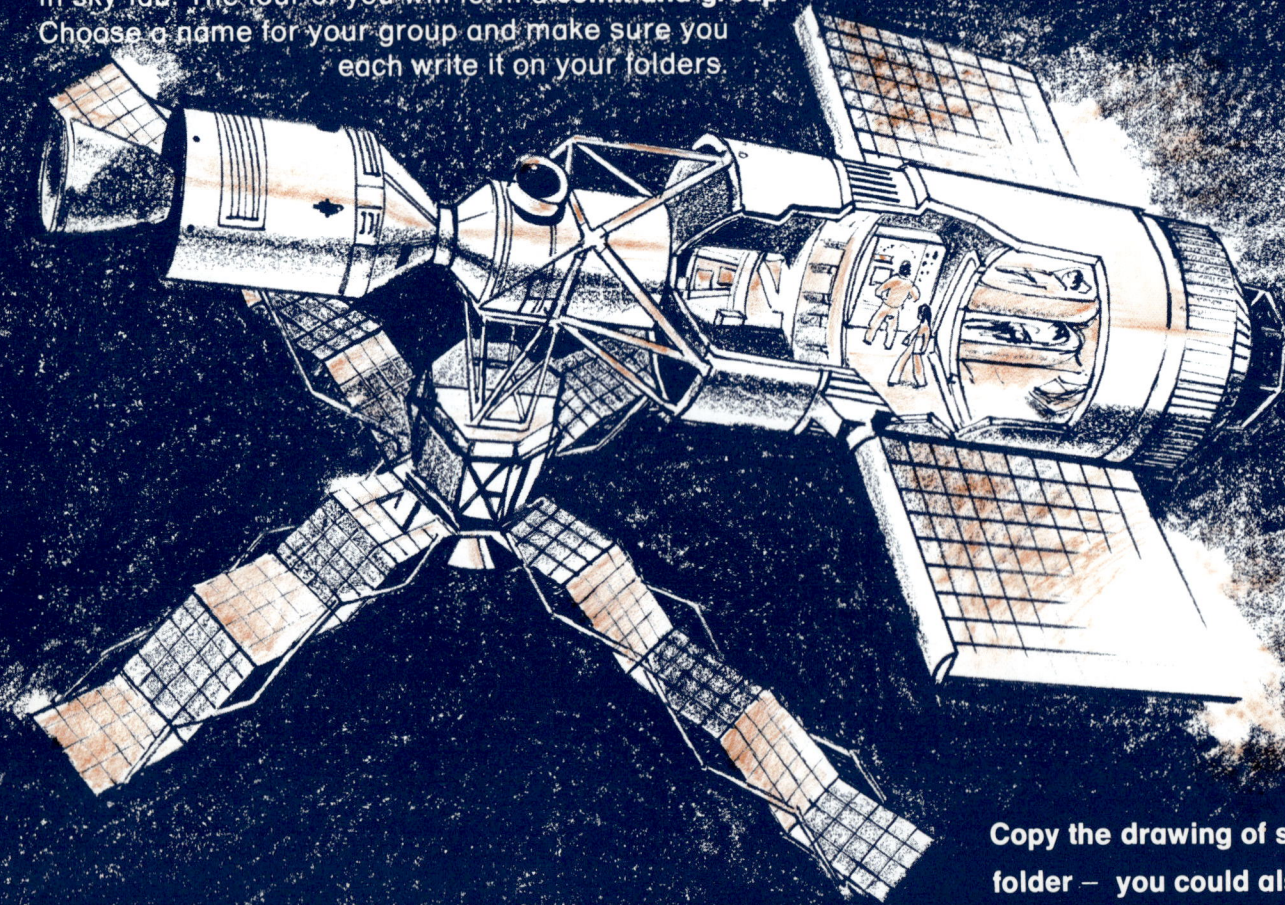

Copy the drawing of sky-lab and put it into your folder — you could also make a model of it!

Blast off!

10-9-8-7-6-5-4-3-2-1

ZERO

Imagine you have just arrived at the sky-lab base and are in the docking port of the command module. You pass through the airlock into the living compartment and meet the rest of your group. Blast off is five minutes away.

The countdown begins! You will never see Earth again.

You are going to be in space for 200 days and then you will arrive on a strange new planet you have never seen before.

How do you feel? What thoughts flash through your mind as the countdown begins? Talk about this with your class and teacher.

Write a report of the take off for Earth control and how you felt. Put the report in your Earth 3000 – Theta folder.

Write a story

Imagine you have been in sky-lab for 2 months.

Write a story about an incident which happens on the space craft. Here are some suggestions of things which could happen but it is more fun to think of your own!

1 On your journey, you have to pass Jupiter. Your ship is pulled towards the planet by its powerful magnetic field.

2 The life support systems fail.

3 An important solar panel is damaged.

4 You pass through a meteorite storm.

Afterwards, read your story to your friends. Keep it in your folder.

Space glossary

In sky-lab and on Theta, you will come across many words and terms which are new. Perhaps you already have! For easy reference, it will be important to keep a list of all the new words and terms you come across and write down their meanings.

Such a list is called a *glossary*.

Here are just a few of the words and terms you will need to include. Arrange the words in alphabetical order in a small notebook (or make your own glossary leaflet by stapling together about 16 pieces of paper). Look up the meaning of the words and write them down. Leave enough space for each letter of the alphabet to add new words as you find them.

meteorite	Moon
solar panel	Neptune
galaxy	Pluto
astronaut	Mars
sun	satellite
planet	orbit
gravity	Venus
Jupiter	star
space-shuttle	sky-lab
Mercury	

Keep your glossary in your space folder.

Remember to make your own glossary for other topics you study, especially if your parents or other children are going to read your work.

The journey

200 days is a long time to be travelling in a rocket through outer space.

Make out a programme for one day in your rocket which includes: meals – radio contact with Earth and other space shuttles – video view time – routine sky-lab checks. Also think about time for exercise and computer checks and games. **Put your daily programme into your folder.**

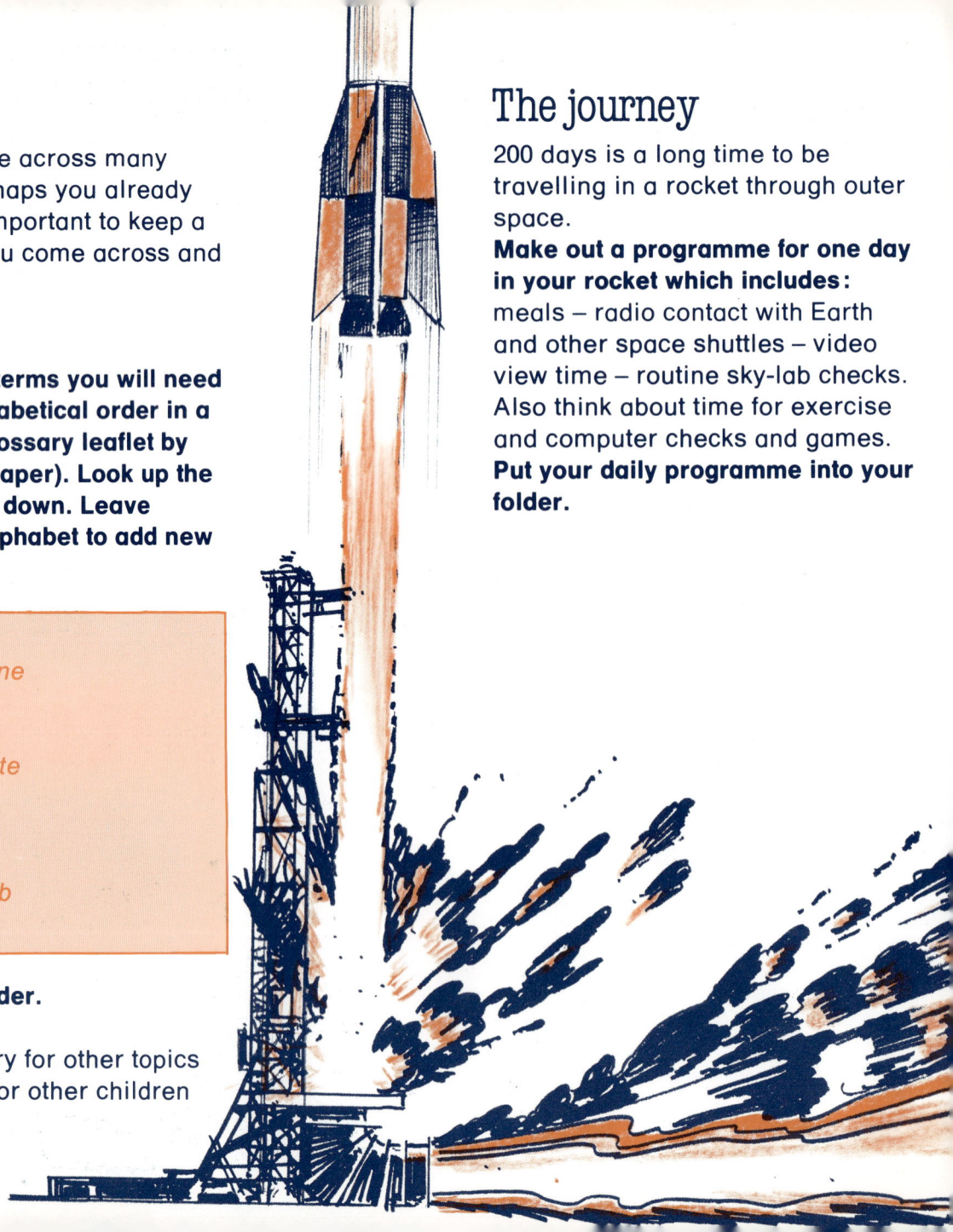

Space clothes

During your time on sky-lab you will experience weightlessness because of the change in gravity. Sometimes you may need to go outside the sky-lab to repair it. You won't be able to breathe the air in outer space. So your clothes will have to be adapted for these conditions.

Here is a drawing of the space suit you would probably wear!

Copy down this drawing and put it into your folder.

Write an account for the sky-lab log, of your space walk to repair the solar panels. Put the account in your folder.

Theta survival gear

Design and draw a costume for a boy or girl of your age which will be suitable for life on Theta.
Remember the climatic conditions on the planet will be different from Earth's.
Add labels to your drawing to explain the costume and its uses.
Keep this drawing in your folder too.

Landing on Theta

Your sky-lab rocket has landed safely on Theta. But you are the first command group to arrive. You contact Earth control and discover that the next rocket won't arrive for another two weeks. You are on your own on a strange new planet.

Discuss with your group, and then with your class and teacher, what it will be like on Theta and how you would feel arriving there.

Write down your ideas about:
– how to provide warm shelter;
– how to provide food;
– how to explore the planet;
– how to relax.

Paint a picture of the planet. Think about what colour it will be and what the landscape will be like. Will there be mountains? Perhaps icebergs? Will there be any vegetation? What will it be like?

Draw a detailed map of the area around your landing base. Mark in any craters and other useful landmarks. Mark the water supply.

Discuss with your group the names you will give to these landmarks and put them on your map, too. Keep the map in your folder. It will be a vital reference once you start to explore the planet.

Cassette data report

Earth command has asked you to record your impressions of your first 24 hours on Theta. The cassette will be stored in sky-lab, played to new arrivals on the planet and copies will be sent to settlers on other planets so they can share your experiences. With your group, work out what information and impressions you think are important to put on cassette and then record them.

Some people from Earth have been re-settled on the Moon. They aren't as lucky as you because they need to carry oxygen tanks to help them breathe and they have to wear heavy lunar boots to keep them on the ground. (Gravity is one third that on Earth.)

Here is a poem by one of the Moon command group members.
How do you think the writer feels? Talk about this with your class. Are you glad you went to Theta?

From the cramped module,
Out to the silence of the moon.
Not a whisper of wind,
Not a whisper of sound,
Just timeless barren blackness.
No colour except a beautiful semi-circle in the sky,
Blues and swirling whites, my home planet, Earth.
In this blackness
Death is dominant.
Yet in this desolate world a life far greater.
The sun shadows,
Half in freezing darkness, half in burning light,
The white planet,
Through the dark-brown fish tank of my visor.
I, the Earthling,
Scan the dead planet.
Katherine Forrest
Now look carefully at the
words which the writer used.
Think about the sounds
which the words make.

Working with a friend, take it in turns to read the poem out loud.
The person who isn't reading must listen very carefully to how the other person sounds.
Was your friend's voice soft or loud?
Did the voice go deeper at any time?
Did your friend read slowly or quickly?
Discuss what you find with your friend. If you have a cassette recorder, record your readings so you can both listen to them together.
Listen to the poem on the cassette which goes with this book.

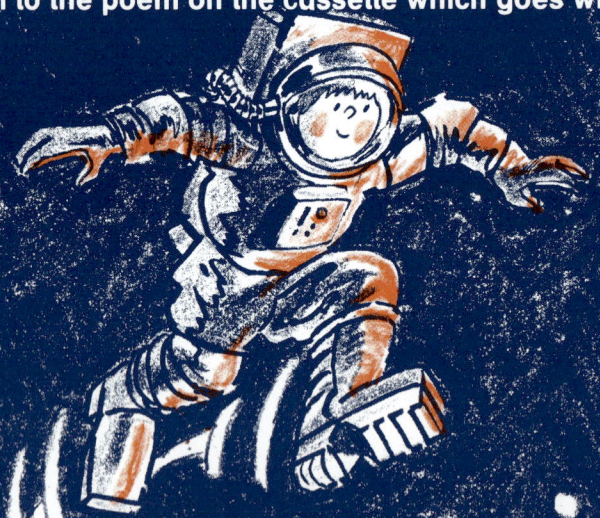

Now it's your turn!

Write a poem using words which have interesting sounds. The sounds of the words should help the meaning of the poem.

Here are some titles to choose from but it is more fun to make up a title of your own:
Lost in space
The planet without lights
Weightlessness in space
Rocket launch
Space lake on Mars
Craters on the Moon
My planet Theta

When you have finished, read your poem to your friend (or ask your friend to read it to you!). How does it sound? Listen to other people reading their poems. Think about how they read their poems.

Moon mime

Imagine, for a minute, that you are on the moon too. It is playtime. Remember that gravity is one third that of Earth so you will be wearing heavy boots to keep you on the ground.

What do you do at playtime? (Remember, if you bounce a ball, it will go three times higher than normal; if you jump up in the air, you will go three times higher, too.)

Life forms on Theta

Will there be any new strange life forms on Theta? If so, what might they be like? How would they have adapted to the conditions on the planet? Would they be friendly?
Draw pictures of three imaginary life forms you might meet on Theta and name them. Put them into your folder.

Write a story

Imagine you go off alone on a space rover to explore Theta.
You meet one of the alien beings you have just drawn.
What happens?

Now read this. It is an extract from a book called *The Heavenly Host* by Isaac Asimov. You will read about a boy called Jonathan Derodin who is faced with the same problem as you. Jonathan has arrived on Planet Anderson with his mother and goes off to explore.

Jonathan was glad he'd been left alone because he wanted to explore. The folder he had read said it was not a dangerous world. It certainly didn't seem so from what he could see.

He and his mother had been given a cabin near the spaceport. All the land around looked very friendly and homelike. The houses were made of a kind of shiney rock that glittered a bit in the yellow sunlight (which seemed a little bit brighter than the sun back home at Ceti Four). Between the houses and all around them it was green. There was grass and shrubs and, farther off fields of grain on low, rolling hills. When he climbed to the top of one of them, he could see a river in the distance.

In the other direction, the green human world stopped. Jon took a road in that direction, and when it stopped, he found the land beyond was made up of rocky ridges. It was then that he saw his first Wheel, one of the native inhabitants of Anderson Two.

He didn't know it was a Wheel, of course, even though the folder had described them. What he saw was just a slab of rock about eight feet high, standing on its narrow edge in the sunlight, like a big figure 1. There didn't seem anything alive about it, but there was nothing else like it anywhere.

He was making up his mind to go closer and see what it was like, when from behind a rock there came another human being. He was looking at the big slab, too, looking so hard he didn't see Jonathan.

The man was inching forward slowly, and then his right arm started to rise and Jonathan saw that he had a blaster in it. It was then that it occurred to Jonathan that the slab must be one of the Wheels he had read about, and before he even thought about it, he was shouting,

"Don't shoot it, mister!" The man with the blaster whirled, his face twisting in surprise. He had a ruddy complexion and fiery red hair. He seemed so astonished at seeing Jonathan that for a moment he simply froze.

In that moment the slab of rock came to life. It broke into a series of bright, flashing lights of various colours coming and going very rapidly. The top third and the bottom third of the slab split into six parts. It seemed suddenly a large hand with six thick fingers at each end. The fingers spread wide, and then it went whirling away like a twelve-spoked wheel, turning end over end so rapidly that it blurred. Jonathan could see now why they were called Wheels.

Why do you think Jonathan shouted to stop the man shooting at the Wheel? What would you have done in the same circumstances and why?
Talk about this with your class and teacher.
Draw a picture of the Wheel and colour it in.

The solar system

Here is a drawing of Earth's solar system with some information about its major planets. Command groups from Earth have been sent to settle on Mars and Pluto (Theta is not in the Earth's solar system).

Jupiter

Earth

Venus

Mercury

Mars

Mercury –
has a surface covered with craters.
There is no air as we know it.
The days are very hot and the nights are extremely cold.

Venus –
a boiling hot, smouldering planet with a bare, rocky landscape. The atmosphere is composed mainly of carbon monoxide which is poisonous to us.

Mars –
dry, dusty and windy. Covered in huge volcanoes, craters and canyons. Much colder than Earth with very thin air.

Uranus

Neptune

Pluto

Saturn

Now do this:
What do you think life will be like for the command groups on Mars and Pluto? Use the information about the planets to write a short account of life on Mars and Pluto for people from Earth.
How will life on Mars and Pluto be different from your life on Theta? Discuss this with your class and teacher.

Invent an alien life form for three of the planets in Earth's solar system and do a drawing or painting of each one. Use the information about each planet to help you decide what the aliens will look like and how they have adapted to survive the conditions on their planet.

Jupiter, Saturn, Uranus and **Neptune** are believed to be globes of gas where no human could survive.

Pluto – freezing cold and dark.

Colonisation of Theta

Your two weeks alone on Theta are over. Today you are expecting four sky-lab rockets to land bringing new people to the planet.
How will you welcome them? Talk about this with your group.

Sort through your **Earth 3000 – Theta** folder and decide what information it will be important for the new settlers to have and why. If there is anything else you think they should know, prepare the information for them.

Write a story

Choose one exciting incident which you think could have happened to you on Theta and write about it. Read it to a friend.

The future

Talk about these questions with your friends and teacher:
How do you see the future for you on Theta?
How will you colonise the planet?
Will you want to keep contact with Earth settlers on other planets?
How will you do this?
Will you visit them?

Here are some things which could happen to you on Theta.
Choose one and write a story about it:

1 Attack by an alien space craft
2 Outbreak of mystery illness
3 Discovery of living plant forms
4 Exploration by space buggy
Make a model of the area around you on Theta.

Now quietly read this poem:

Walking in space

Waiting, listening, nothingness.
All around eternity stretched.
Lovely crystal colours drifting,
Kingdom of silence.
Infinity.
Nothingness
Going on and on.

I am floating on a moonbeam,
No top or bottom, no left or right.

So still.
Perhaps a new dimension.
All is so serene, so
Calm,
Everlasting space.
Adam Coombes

Would you really like to leave planet Earth?

63

Bibliography

Here is a list of stories about some of the themes in this book.
This list will help you to find the books easily in your local
library.
The author's name comes first followed by the title of the book
and then the publishers.

Feeling scared
DICKINSON, P. *Annerton Pit*. Puffin
DICKINSON, S. *Ghostly experiences*. Lion
ELLIOT, M. *Witch's gold*. Abelard
GARFIELD, L. *Devil-in-the-fog*. Constable Young Books
        The ghost downstairs. Puffin
GRAY, N. S. *Grimbold's other world*. Faber & Faber
HOKE, H. *Creepies*. Franklin Watts
        Terrors, traumas and terrors. J. M. Dent
IRESON, B. *Creepy creatures*. Beaver
        Haunting tales. Puffin
MACE, E. *The ghost diviners*. Deutsch
SNYDER, Z. K. *A witch in the family*. Beaver

Without words
KING, C. *Stig of the Dump*. Puffin
MARSHALL, J. VANCE. *Walkabout*. Puffin

About outer space
FISK, N. *A rag, a bone and a hank of hair*. Kestrel
        Escape from Splatterbang. Pelham
        Monster maker. Pelham
        Time trap. Gollancz
        Trillions. Hamish Hamilton
HEINLEIN, R. A. *Have space will travel*. Gollancz
        Tunnel in the sky. Gollancz
        Farmer in the sky. Gollancz
        Red planet. Gollancz
        Time for the stars. Gollancz

MOORE, P. *The moon raiders*. Armada
        Spy in space. Armada
        Planet of fear. Armada
NORTON, A. *Outside*. Blackie
The Dr Who series published by W. H. Allen

**The authors and publishers would also like to thank the following
illustrators and photographers:**
Rowan Clifford – page 13
John Freeman – page 24
Tony Garrett – page 25
Julia Hutton – pages 4, 10, 12, 14, 32, 38
Shirley McLaughlin – pages 5, 8, 15, 16, 18, 20, 21, 26, 27, 28, 30, 31
Colin Mier – pages 5, 6, 17, 29, 43
Kate Penoyre – pages 24, 40, 42, 43
Pilot Photography – cover
John Shackell – pages 48–63
Janine Weidel – pages 44, 45
Woman's Own – page 7
With thanks also to *British Rail* and the *BBC Radio Times* for their help with
this project, and the Royal National Institute for the Deaf for permission to
reproduce material from the booklet *Sign and Say*.